ADULTS ONLY

For People Who Love Their Country More Than Their Party

Sid Dinerstein

FIRST EDITION

Brenda Star, Development Director
Shawn McAllister, Editor
Mel Abfier, Creative Director
Terry van Rhyn, Illustrator
Jane Evers, Marketing Manager

StarGroup International, Inc.
West Palm Beach, Florida
561.547.0667
wwww.stargroupinternational.com

Printed in USA

Library of Congress Cataloging-in-Publication Data Pending

Adults Only - Sid Dinerstein

ISBN 978-1-884886-86-7

This book is available at:
• local book stores
• amazon.com
• siddinerstein.com
• 1.888.281.5170
Customized bulk orders (1,000 minimum) are available by contacting:

StarGroup International
1194 Old Dixie Highway
Suite 201
West Palm Beach, FL 33403
(561) 547-0667

www.stargroupinternational.com

Table of Contents

Foreword

The United States has a caring national conscience. She has always been alert to the injustices and inequities that inevitably arise in any human institution and has always been at the forefront to eliminating immoral and unjust practices.

We enter the 21st century facing some of the biggest threats in our nation's history. The new millennium with its space age technology brings with it monumental challenges and obstacles from both outside forces whose primary objective is to annihilate America and destroy the American way of life and from inside circumstances that are leading to a path of self destruction. Sid Dinerstein describes the major issues confronting America in the 21st century and has succinctly and articulately mapped out the necessary strategy we need to adopt in order to overcome these challenges.

By the grace of God and our forefathers who drafted the U.S. Constitution, we are also a nation of people with a monumental responsibility of free will to ensure that the principles of justice, equality, and independence shall persevere. Free people in a free society have a choice. It's time to choose America's future. We can choose to re-establish the direction our forefathers intended for us or we can continue with the status quo and face the consequences. We *can* fix what is wrong. We *must* fix what is wrong. Dinerstein effectively shows us how. It's a risk, but it's a risk we must be willing to take in order to survive. The only political or economic system in which there is no risk is one in which there also is no choice. If we forget that, we lose everything.

Every generation must learn anew to appreciate the rights and privileges that America provides. It's time for today's generation to step up to the plate. Sid Dinerstein leads the way.

Rich DeVos

Introduction

This wasn't my idea.

The thought of writing a book was the last thing on my mind. I'm not a writer. (There's a line for the book reviewers). I'm a full-time volunteer with School Boards, Girls' sports coaching, politics, buses, country clubs and tennis; not necessarily in that order. My fun time is with all the women in my life... my wife, Esther... my daughters, Staci and Jodi... and Jodi's and Douglas' daughters, Leah and Becca.

Now I'm writing a book. I guess it could be worse. People are always telling me to run for public office. I decided to write a book instead.

My political activities require that I do a lot of public speaking. I'm constantly told that I can "connect the dots" ... finding the causes of and solutions to vexing problems. I hope it's not too immodest to say: "I agree." Eventually, the perfect storm occurred. The urgings of my friends, the concerns of the electorate and the pressure from Brenda, my publisher, came together to put this book in your hands.

The American Century should be, but probably won't be, the 21st century. We need to "renew our vows" that were affirmed by our Declaration of Independence's "all men are created equal," and by our Constitution's "We the people."

I chose the title *"**Adults Only**"* because it puts a very long message into two simple words. Our lives are a constant stream of denials, "whatever's" and kicking cans down the road instead of tackling today's problems today. Those problems can be losing weight, paying off credit cards or paying off the national debt... they're all major problems that we are very good at avoiding.

Whether or not you agree with a single word I write, you'll have to agree I touch a lot of sensitive nerves.

Frankly, it's all about the children. *We* need to grow up before *they* do. And our government needs to grow up while we're still fat and happy. Nothing lasts forever.

Sid Dinerstein

Adults Only

merica is over 230 years old. On July 4, 1776, our founding fathers produced the Declaration of Independence that said *all men are created equal*. By 1789, we ratified a Constitution that started with the words, *We The People*. America to this day is the greatest social experiment in the history of mankind. It's been successful beyond probably anybody's prediction. We are not just successful in all the material ways, we are a great and noble people. Let me make this clear to the rest of the world… if there was no America, the rest of the world would be less. They had a choice to either become part of civilization or lose all their best citizens to us because we raised the bar. People from all nations flocked to our country. They still do. We built a country that has become large, that says if you work hard, if you are creative, if you are productive, you have an opportunity to take care of yourself and your family in ways that you couldn't dream of anywhere else on the planet. We had a very limited central government and a very engaged populous. We took this country to war in the 19th century because the vision that was laid out in the 18th century still had gaps. It is a work in progress that continues to this day. We went to war in the 19th century because a whole segment of the population wasn't able to vote.

In 1920, less than 90 years ago, the 19th Amendment was passed giving women the right to vote. Later, we lowered the voting age to 18. In 1990, other rights were extended to the handicapped and disabled members of American society. We have a right to believe in the "Shining City on the Hill."

Today, the *bounce* is out of our step. The *swagger* is out of our walk. Polls indicate that three-quarters of our citizens say we're headed in the wrong direction. A majority say our best days are behind us. Angst is our national emotion. Blame is the political strategy of choice. Thirty percent of registered voters today are neither Democrats nor Republicans. Who can blame them? If that isn't enough to scare members of both national parties, then they're just not paying attention. We take delight in keeping either party from solving anything, lest someone says something good about them.

"We the people" are now "We the children"

What happened is that during its long 230+-year journey, our government changed... but our Constitution didn't. Once upon a time we had a barely notice-able federal budget. Today, we have a multi-trillion-dollar money machine. The humble electees have become today's keepers of the purse strings. "We the people" are now "We the children." The "consent of the governed" has become the "begging for the bacon."

Americans are complex people. We are generous, engaging and optimistic. Yet like all people, we also have the capacity to be selfish, power hungry and narcissistic. If you want to see both sides of good people, take a look at your close friends going through a divorce. You will ask, "How can two of the nicest people in the world become those two people?" The people we elect, our Presidents, our Congressmen, our Senators, are just like us. They're fundamentally bright, decent and caring. Once upon a time... and maybe to this day... they ran for those jobs to make the world a better place. But today's incentives are perverse. The people we elect, bright-eyed, bushy-tailed Congressmen, Senators and Presidents, go off to Washington and they find heaven. They find good money, staff, perks, power and people kissing their ring on a daily basis. Between the cocktail parties, golf outings, foreign travel and media interviews, the first priority of the newbie

Unlimited Spending + Infinite Lobbyists = 40 Years of Washington

is to get a lifetime ticket. Enter the lobbyists... line them up, hold your fund raisers, and you're on your way to a 40-year, very cool gig.

Oh, as far as those problems that we sent them there to solve... "Well, if it wasn't for those mean people in the other party, we would be well on our way. And as soon as the public kicks out all of the other people on the other side, we'll work on it. In the meantime, there's a corporate jet waiting for me."

Indeed, I call it the Forever Formula. The Forever Formula is:

Unlimited Spending + Infinite Lobbyists = 40 years of Washington

We, the *real* people, pay all the bills and alternate between digging in and tuning out. Then we go off to the mall.

So, now we all agree. There's something wrong. We don't debate... we scream and insult. Everyone's right and wrong at the same time. Our word of choice is "whatever." Well, I'm here to say (with great modesty), "Cheer up, America. Help is on the way. In just a few minutes, you're going to understand the problem and the solution."

We grew up to become children. As our country matured, our citizens regressed. "We the people" became "we the children," and the electees became "they the parents." We bicker about the relationship between the Executive and the Legislative and the Judiciary. We bicker between D's and R's... Democrats and Republicans. We really need a *fight* between the "I's" and the "O's." They're the "I's" – the Insiders. We're the "O's" – the Outsiders.

Now, with too many problems and not enough answers comes the *Adults Only* Trilogy — the three Amendments to the United States Constitution that will make the 21st century America's *best*. They're all what I call 80 percenters. As you go across America, 80 percent of the people will agree with all three of the things I'm about to say. And 80 percent of the elected people in Washington will disagree. Here they are:

Amendment #1: TERM LIMITS

Amendment #2: A BALANCED BUDGET

Amendment #3: ENGLISH AS OUR OFFICIAL LANGUAGE

Term Limits

The concept is simple. It's four, two-year terms for a Congressman and two, six-year terms for a Senator. The effects are profound. Everybody who gets elected is able to bring his or her expertise to the issues at hand, to take a seat in Congress, to negotiate and legislate and compromise and do what we ask him to do. Lifers need not apply. That's the thing about term limits. The 40-year guys don't need to show up. They've got to find new gigs somewhere else in the world that will pay them that kind of money for that little work. Good luck.

With term limits we ask citizens to come for a brief period to solve specific problems for which their career accomplishments have prepared them.

Balanced Budgets

The difficult part of the Trilogy is the Balanced Budget Amendment. This one is hard. My Balanced Budget Amendment is not like any that they talk about in Washington. It's an *Adults Only* Balanced Budget Amendment... the kind that children like us are not supposed to know about. Here's what everybody needs to understand: when they talk about Balanced Budget Amendments, they say things like, "We have an annual deficit of about 200 billion dollars a year. We're going to either raise taxes or cut programs, or do a combination of the two. We're going to get that down to zero and we're going to have a balanced budget." However, the truth is you won't even have a half balanced budget.

Every year the national debt increases over 500 billion dollars — half a trillion dollars a year, 1.44 billion dollars a day, seven days a week, 365 days a year. How come if the deficit is 200 *billion* dollars, the debt increases 500 *billion* dollars? In 2006, we had an accumulated debt of eight-and-a-half billion dollars. In 2007, we have a deficit of

200 billion dollars. You would think we would have an accumulated debt at the end of the year of $8.7 billion, but in fact, it was already at 9 billion by September of 2007. How does this happen? This happens because so many projects are placed "Off Budget." Hurricane Katrina devastated New Orleans. Congress and the President are going to chip in 100 billion dollars to help them rebuild that town, and we say "OK." Where's it coming from? The answer is, *nowhere*. It's Off Budget. That means that it doesn't change the 200 billion dollars one bit. But it adds 100 billion dollars to next year's debt. It's *Off* the budget and *On* the debt. Nice! See the "US National Debt Clock" for yourself at brillig.com. The President goes around the world and visits a country that we once heard of, and is now back in the news for some reason or another. He announces an agreement, in-cluding Loan Forgiveness. Everybody heard of those words? *Loan Forgiveness*. We used to do Foreign Aid. We now do Loan Forgiveness. We make them loans that they have no chance of repaying, and then many years down the road we forgive them for it. It's Off Budget. If you forgive them 20 billion dollars in loans, you've just increased the national debt by 20 billion dollars, even though you haven't touched the annual budget deficit.

Democracy is not a spectator sport

The **Adults Only** Balanced Budget Constitutional Amendment reads as follows:

The cumulative national debt may not increase from one year to the next. (An exception may be made only for a declared war with Congressional approval.)

That is not a "no new tax" position. It is not a "no new spending" position. It is a position that says the people who go to Washington have to make the hard choices concerning the allocation of limited resources. When they come up with a new program that costs a hundred dollars, it has to come from somewhere. You then wind up with *real* adults having *real* discussions over <u>real</u> problems... the same way that you do over the kitchen table when all of a sudden you have an emergency in your family, and you need to have that extra thousand dollars. That is central to this position. The reason why Term Limits are necessary, but not sufficient, is that if term limited electees still had this unlimited checkbook, we would still be kicking this fiscal can down the road. All 50 states have to balance their budget every year. Special Legislative sessions are convened when they come up short. They don't have an *Off Budget* option and some are *Term Limited*. They all have to negotiate in good faith and come up with solutions that everybody can live with.

English as our official language

We all came from somewhere else. Each new immigrant group added to our culture with unique words, fabulous foods and a great work ethic. The common goals were Opportunity and Assimilation. That meant speaking English and dollars. Ao long as there were many cultures, English was essential. Now that there is one other extraordinarily large culture... the Hispanic culture... English is even more essential. In Canada, they have friends and "amis" – and Separation referenda. If we have friends and "amigos," our "e pluribus" will stop becoming "unum." More on this later where a comprehensive immigration program is presented that deals with all those current issues.

In an Adult Only world, there is one overriding truth – *Democracy is not a spectator sport.* You cannot talk about *Adults Only* and then leave it to everybody else to make the decisions that have profound effects on you, your children and your grandchildren. Everybody in the country has to have some involvement, more than an occasional trip to a voting booth to vote for the party their parents told them to vote for. Most don't even know what each party is about.

Somebody needs to go to America and say, "I understand why we're not what we used to be." If we are going to have a 21st century that is once again an American century, we must become young and vibrant again, and unclog our hardened arteries. We all have the same needs. No matter which political party we support, no matter which church, synagogue, book club, current events group, service organization or whatever we belong to, we all

> The fiscal can that we're kicking down the road is going to hit a bump, come up and smack us in the head

have the same concerns and the same fears. Everybody asks, "Why can't we get better people to run for high public office?" The truth is there are pretty good people on both sides. But the incentives that now exist make the chances close to zero of getting much accomplished in Washington today.

We could all live with the other party if they didn't have blank checks and unlimited time in Washington. That's exactly the point. It's time to think about our new old relationship. It's about changing the discussion to I versus O… the Insiders versus the Outsiders. This is about giving our country a 21st century that right now the insiders are giving away. You cannot have a 9 trillion dollar debt, unfunded entitlements in the 20-30 trillion dollar range and expect a happy ending. Life isn't like that. The fiscal can that we're kicking down the road is going to hit a bump, come up and smack us in the head. We know it's going to happen, but more than that, we know we can fix it.

We need to make sure that our government grows up before our grandchildren do. Prepare yourself to get involved. We've got work to do.

We need to make sure that our government grows up before our grandchildren do

It's The All You Can Eat Weight Loss Secret

That was fun. We all got to bash the government. Bashing government is not only fun, it's a sport. It's the ultimate American sport. My intent is to take everybody out of their comfort zone and hold up a mirror to all of us. When we do that, what America sees is a lot of overweight, under-exercised Americans. And what are they doing? Well, they're driving to the bookstore to buy the latest diet book. We will never be adult enough to take back our government if we're not adult enough to take back our own lives. The two are inextricably entwined.

It's more fun being children. It's always more fun being children. We all know that. Consider one of my favorite examples of how great it is to be a child. We can eat Danish and rolls for breakfast and call it cake. You see? This is a great thing. Only in America can you do stuff like that. Every diet book should have the same title. They should call it the "All You Can Eat" book, because that's why we buy it. They tell us you can *have it all*. You can do Atkins... you can do the bacon... and the steak... and the fries... and the ice cream. I have a friend who's been doing this for years. He'll never lose weight. Who's kidding whom? While the diet book people really do want you to read and grow thin, we must never forget that they're in the *book* business, not the *diet* business. They don't get paid by the pound... they get paid by the book. They need you to buy their book more than they need you to lose weight.

The nightmare of the diet book business is that everyone would learn the two-word Adult Only weight loss secret: Grow Up. That's because when we grow up, when our inner adult takes over from our inner child, we're finished with diet books, diet fads, gastric bypasses, liposuction and other 21st century immature processes. We're ready for the next two-word weight loss secret... a really big one: Eat Less. You don't have to know more than that. You can read every book that was ever published, and, trust me, if you eat less you will lose weight. You don't have to do the science. It doesn't mean that some foods, aren't better than other foods and some foods aren't worse. Eating *less* doesn't mean eating French Fries for breakfast, lunch and dinner with a side of cake. The fact is you don't have to be fanatical. You just have to eat less. For many people in America, the sad truth is that eating less means eating *a lot* less... like 50 to 75 percent.

> # We grew up to become children

One thing which is interesting about America is *good* news. We have the cheapest food in the world. I don't mean just fast food. I mean if you take the cost of feeding ourselves and our families as a percentage of our paychecks, there's no country in the world that comes close. That has a lot to do with free trade and good farming.

The *bad* news is we don't eat... we graze. I graze. You graze. We all graze. You know what I mean? We just go around and we have popcorn in the middle of the day and, do all these wonderful things that put a smile on our face and a couple of hundred more calories in our belly.

When we eat less, we feel healthier, physically and mentally. Our improved attitude and self confidence bring us back to our *Adults Only* mission, which is to take back the government. The *best* news is that you can be an adult in government affairs or personal affairs. Either one gets you to the other. This is an essential point. If you're ready for either, you're ready for both. If you can live a healthy lifestyle that includes less food, enough exercise, moderate alcohol, no cigarettes and all-the-time seatbelts, then you're ready to take back your government. Conversely, if you're able to understand the perverse incentives that take us from "We the people" to "We the children" in our government... and you're ready, willing and able to take that on... then the bonus is you're ready to clean up your personal act. It's one of these really interesting things. It's the same all the time. It doesn't matter whether you're the chicken or the egg. You get to win as soon as you do either. Another way that I like to say it: "This is the bicycle syndrome. Once you learn it, you never forget."

Which state in the country is going to be the first to pass our three constitutional amendments – term limits, balanced budgets, English as the official language? Colorado. Why Colorado? Because they're the skinniest state in America. That means they're ready! There are more people there who *are ready* to do *adult things* because they've already taken charge of their lives. I lost over 30 pounds in 1979. Losing weight is arguably the hardest thing that you do in your life. Once you do that, taking on the government and amending the constitution kind of comes easy.

You can't have an *Adults Only* discussion of personal health without the equally important and much more difficult discussion of health issues and health insurance. Let's start with a bowl of spaghetti.

Health Insurance

3

Of Course I Want It.
It's Covered

I f you look at a bowl of spaghetti, the American healthcare system looks right back at you. Spaghetti is the perfect food to leap from Wellness to *Healthcare*. Too much spaghetti, something we all want, makes us bigger.

Trying to find a loose end to separate the pieces seems unlikely. *Healthcare* coverage in America is a continual tug of war involving private sector employers, public sector employers, private insurers, government insurance programs, doctors, lawyers, lobbyists, lawyer lobbyists and the lonely victims whom we call *patients*. Indeed, the only people not at the table are our children and our grandchildren — heirs to the multi-trillion dollar promises we made for Medicare and Medicaid programs. The best thing we can say about our healthcare coverage in America is that it's not like all the others. We don't send seniors home to die. We don't have 18-month waiting lists for surgery and six-month waiting lists for doctor's appointments. We don't have a nine percent unemployment rate. We don't have a 70-percent tax rate. Other than that, we have a *mess*.

Our system was brought to us by the Japanese. Yes, on December 7, 1941, the wage and price controls of World War II encouraged employers to add perks to keep and attract employees. Voila! Health insurance. We overlaid that with bundles of money called Medicaid and Medicare, and forgot to add the Fraud Detection Unit. But mostly healthcare in America is a spaghetti bowl of programs, because every piece of legislation further violates a fundamental *Adults Only* rule which is: Costs are controlled when the *patient* is the payer. In other words, we negotiate for our own money, but we say: "I'll do it if it's covered"... when someone else is paying the bill. Adults know that getting immediate medical attention from the world's best doctors, in the world's best health facilities, followed by prescriptions for the world's best wonder drugs, costs money. Children think Covered means Free.

> ## Healthcare costs are controlled when the patient is the payer

An *Adults Only* healthcare coverage program requires term-limited elected officials and our *Adults Only* balanced budget. Once we remove the undue influence of the lobbyists and the powerful seduction of massive deficit spending, we can actually do some good.

My eight point *Adults Only* Healthcare solution to this mess in America is:

- Minimum health insurance deductible of $5,000. Above that, everything's covered.

- Mandated free periodic physicals and appropriate shots and tests

- Rates adjusted by "wellness" based on age and health

- Policies sold nationally, not just within the state that you live

- Pain and suffering awards capped at three times damages

- Small business can buy cooperationally

- Small business can self insure with a catastrophe override

- Medicaid and Medicare members are part of the Fifty-Cent Rebate Program. That means any unused portion of their $5,000 deductible gets the patient a check at the end of the year for half of the unused portion. Private employers should want to follow that

Let me explain the eight points:

Number one – health insurance is not supposed to cover the routine visits to the doctor because the baby is running a temperature. With a $5,000 deductible in both private and government programs, all patients will price shop, and all prices will fall.

Number two – we shouldn't be paying for masectomies because someone forgot to get the mammogram. You want coverage, you get tested. A $200 mammogram beats a $20,000 breast removal in every way. And guys, that means that someone is going to put a scope where the sun doesn't shine, because we're all *Adults Only*.

Number three – Smokers and overweight couch potatoes: If you want to be a grown-up child, pay for the privilege. My father-in-law was covered so well he never adjusted his diet, never sped up his sedentary lifestyle, never worried about the near zero cost for his 22 pills a day. His stroke was devastating in every way, the money being the least of it. My father-in-law's no longer here. On my daily visit to my mom in the nursing home, I see severed limbs and useless limbs, victims of diabetes, stroke and a healthcare system with perverse incentives; mega dollars for cure, pennies for prevention.

17

Number four – policies sold nationally means more sellers for the same buyers; lower prices, more choices, more competition. All good.

Number five – pain and suffering. When it comes to healthcare, we all have pain and suffering. It's fine for the lawyers to share. They can't just dish out pain and suffering. They have to absorb some of their own.

Number six – small businesses needs friends and associates to buy larger and pay less. It's simple *Adults Only* economics.

Number seven – small businesses can self insure. It's quite simple, and it actually reduces insurance costs if you're a big enough small business.

Number eight –the new concept is the Medicaid/Medicare Fifty-Cent Rebate Program. It goes like this: These members also have a $5,000 deductible making them price-cutting front line warriors. At the end of the year, the government — either Medicaid or Medicare — rebates 50 percent of the unused $5,000 deductible. For example, use $1,000, leave $4,000. Get a check at the end of the year for $2,000. I hear those prices dropping already. Indeed, since the taxpayers spend $7,300 per recipient, the *Fifty Cent* solution has huge promise for everybody. It's an *Adults Only* solution instead of just kicking the fiscal can down the road a few more years. My *Adults Only* healthcare program is both creative and requires term-limited Congressmen and a balanced budget spending discipline. It is truly for *Adults Only*.

Any discussion of Medicaid and Medicare leads to the larger discussion of entitlements and the single biggest financial threat to our children, our grandchildren and our country.

I'm Entitled

I'm *entitled* to get Social Security from age 62 until the day I die. I'm *entitled* to massive subsidies for my healthcare through Medicare until the day I die. I'm *entitled*... I'm *entitled*... I'm *entitled*.

Well how about this? You're not entitled to bankrupt the national treasury. You're not entitled to impoverish your grandchildren. And you're not entitled to stop all reasonable attempts at reform. Entitlements are the whole enchilada. Entitlements are the number one reason that an *Adults Only* solution must be discussed *and* turned into viable legislation. Entitlements are the fiscal elephants sitting right in the middle of our national living room. So if you're not ready for raw, hard, *Adults Only* entitlement facts and figures, skip the next paragraphs, the ones with all the numbers. But for the hardcore *Adults Only* frontline warriors in the battle for the soul of our government, here goes:

Medicare covers 43 million Americans at an annual cost of $374 billion, representing about 14 percent of our budget, but not 14 percent of our national debt. It is financed by an employer/employee 2.9 percent payroll tax combination. Medicare currently runs at an annual deficit. What that means is that all the people in this country go to work and get their paycheck with the Medicare deduction. That does not cover the amount of money that seniors are currently using just for their healthcare. That's how bad it is, because the *real* seniors, the Baby Boomers who are getting older, haven't stepped up to the window yet.

There is NO MONEY in the Social Security fund – period

Social Security covers 48 million Americans at an annual cost of over $500 billion. That's half a trillion, the same as our annual increased annual debt, at an average of $10,500 per recipient. Social Security is financed by an employee/employer 15 percent payroll tax combination. Social Security runs at an annual surplus of about $114 billion. That means that all the money that goes in is about $114 billion more than all the checks that are written. The most important *Adults Only* facts are these:

- There is <u>*NO MONEY*</u> in the Social Security fund — *period*.

- There's no bank account with your name on it waiting for your retirement.

- There are *no earnings* on the trillions of Social Security dollars taken from our paychecks over the last 40 years.

We do not have to wait for Social Security to go broke. It went broke in 1968, the day Congress voted to take the Social Security surplus into our regular budget. That's when Social Security went from being a retirement fund to the national chain letter... wages being put in weekly and benefits being mailed out monthly. In exchange, we put in IOU's... *really*, like the kind a child would put in his piggy bank after he emptied it to buy the latest Webkinz. Most of you don't know what Webkinz are, but grandparents do.

Bear with me. The worst is yet to come. Our combined unfunded commitment for Social Security and Medicare is $36 trillion. That's trillion with one T, two L's and TWELVE ZEROS. Add in our $9 trillion current debt obligation and we're on the hook for $45 trillion. This is all true. But of course there are 300 million of us. Think of it this way. We're on the hook for $375,000 per worker, or more modestly, $150,000 for every man, woman and child in America. That should make you feel better. Ouch!

I went to a baby shower recently, I brought an IOU. I'm just kidding, but trust me, I could have. Here's something that *is* true. When I told my seven-year-old granddaughter, Leah, I was writing a book, she asked the title. I said: "*Adults Only*." She got very sad. She said she wouldn't

Congress made promises that we could not keep and cannot break

be able to read it because she's only a child. I told her: "Read it anyway. Just skip the chapter on entitlements."

Now for the good news. The day we have term-limited Congressmen focusing on our *Adults Only* balanced budget, we will all sober up. My *Adults Only* Entitlement Solution Program can only be enacted by term-limited electees, because voting for my program will cost some of them their jobs. Career politicians would never vote for this solution. That's why we need to end Congress as a career. Remember, the old Congress made promises that we could not keep and cannot break. It will take an *Adults Only* Congress to break those promises and return us to solvency.

There are a number of choices about how to eat this elephant. There's the "raise the contribution" option. There's the "cut the benefit" option. And there's the always popular "tax the rich" option. I found myself influenced by three separate images. The first one came, quite literally, when I looked out the window. You see, I live on a golf course in Florida. Yes, lucky me. Aside from the beautiful fairways, the white egrets and the blue herons, I noticed something else; human beings divided into two distinct species. One species drove in golf carts, carried clubs and chased those dimpled golf balls around the course until they found their way into the hole on the green. The other species drove on lawnmowers and cut the grass. Like a bolt out of the blue, I had an epiphany. I realized that every Friday we took money out of the paychecks of the poor grass cutters, and once a month sent that money to the rich golfers. My second influence came from running the numbers. My cousin Alison graduated from college last year and she's out earning a living and building a life. Under today's laws, if Alison works until she's 65 and lives until she's 80, she will collect a fraction of what she and her employer contribute to Social Security. In other words, the younger you are, the more of your wealth is being destroyed by this program.

Number three is Mom. Mom is in the fastest-growing demographic group in the country, the 90 somethings. I visit her every day at a lovely nursing home where she is well cared for. Mom is bright, engaging, energetic and very much enjoying life. And believe me, she's more mobile in her wheelchair than she was with her walker. Mom is a Social Security Jackpot Winner. And, as she likes to remind people, she's very good at Bingo, too. She worked on and off throughout her adult life; much of it was part time. Her Social Security contributions were at small amounts on low wages with small rates. Dad died 12 years ago, but also earned modestly. Mom has been collecting for almost 30 years, currently at almost $1,500 a month. It's the Social Security jackpot – low wages, low Social Security taxes, 30 years of high benefits. Mom and Alison are 180 degrees apart in the Social Security contribution/return matrix.

So here goes, the *Adults Only* Entitlement Reform Program:

- Social Security benefits start at age 75.

- The benefit age is indexed to life expectancy minus three years.

- All Social Security contributions are lock-boxed and untouchable by Congress. We go back to what they took away in '68. Separating out the surpluses and running them to age 75, they become massive.

- Medicare remains unchanged – 65 years of age, including our new Fifty-Cent Rebate Program. If a 65+ senior is working and his employer offers health insurance, he must use that instead of Medicare.

- All federal employment related taxes… income, Social Security and Medicare… end at age 65.

- All federal income taxes on Social Security earnings are repealed.

There I said it. Nobody else will. Those of you who are not *Adults Only* can burn this book. Those who are can start the debate.

Here is some further clarification:

- When Social Security started in 1935, life expectancy was 65. Today it's 78. So 75 is more generous today than 65 was then.

- Indexing makes sense. If 65 had been indexed back in 1935, we wouldn't have this entitlement problem.

- It is essential that we lock the Society Security box with an

Adults Only balanced budget amendment.

- By leaving Medicare alone, medical emergencies remain covered.

- Eliminating federal taxes on seniors will encourage them to work and employers to hire them first. This is a good thing for everyone.

There should never have been taxes on Social Security earnings.

Literally, I can see trillions of dollars in unfunded obligations withering away right before our eyes. As for the Republicans out there, the transition cost to personal accounts are just too long, too much and too hard to get done. To the Democrats out there, every day that there is no reform is another day our children and grandchildren grow poorer.

Entitlements are the fiscal elephants sitting right in the middle of our national living room

---

Voting Is For Old People

How did Social Security and Medicare get that way? Forty-five trillion dollars is a lot of money. It takes 300,000 years to count from one to 45 trillion at 300 words per minute, 24/7. The key historical milestones are the income tax, the graduated income tax and the withholding for the graduated income tax. Someone observed that the fatal flaw of democracy is that at some point, the citizens discover they could vote themselves the national treasury. When they did it in our country in the 20th century, we wound up with lifetime Congressmen and no ceiling on our budget. During the 2000 presidential election, a young woman was interviewed on MTV about her choice for president. Her response was, "Voting is for old people." Sure it is. She votes ten times a week for the American Idol and never for the American President. For that she gets a new celebrity to coo over and a $45 trillion bag full of IOU's. When everybody's in the game except one group, guess who gets stuck with the tab?

I occasionally get to speak to young, politically interested people, ages 18 to 30. My message is always the same. "Don't listen to everyone who says you're the future. Listen to me. I say the future is now. Your 18 birthday doesn't mean you can vote. It means you can run. And run you better if you want a life as good as your parents'."

A young friend of mine who gets this whole thing is a guy named Jeffery. When Jeffery was 18, he ran for the Palm Beach County School Board. That might not sound like a lot, but the Palm Beach County School District has 170,000 kids, 20,000 employees and a $3.5 billion budget. Jeffery got 22 percent of the vote, forcing the other two people to have a run off. Undeterred, a couple of years later, Jeffrey found a Soil and Conservation district. He filed to run and did not draw an opponent. I have to tell you that for young people who think that *being cool* is the next iPod, I think it's way cooler to be the guy raising and spending our tax dollars. And that's what my friend Jeffery does. Go Jeffrey!

> ## Our young people will vote ten times a week for the American Idol and never once for the American President

There are other nationally known people who are relatively young. Louisiana elected a 36-year-old governor named Bobby Jindal. In the State of Florida, Speaker of the House Marco Rubio is only 36-years-old. These are young people who were standing out rather than hanging out in their early 20's or late teens, and they both now have great futures. Believe me, we need them at this point more than they need us. So I say to young people: "Get in the game while you still have some skin, because we need more Adult adults. After all, we gave you a $45 trillion bag full of IOU's, a 50 percent divorce rate and two political parties that barely speak the same language. Surely you can do better than that."

Speaking of the unfunded national debt and the divorce rates, have you figured out the connection yet?

Family Structure

Who's Your Daddy?

*T*he War on Poverty in the 60's had the perverse, unintended consequences of giving regular paychecks to families so long as they do not acquire two specific items: husbands and jobs — and that created a permanent underclass that exists to this day. Poverty and crime mushroomed. Male self-esteem plummeted. It took 30 years, to 1998, to reform those welfare rules and to end lifetime dependency.

The single biggest negative dynamic in America in the past 40 years is the breakup of the family. Divorce rates are 50 percent. We have a 40 percent poverty rate for single-mother-headed households. Indeed, the *Adults Only* Iron Law of Families is: "There is not enough money on the planet to save a community without fathers." And by the way, the same would be true for a community without mothers, but we just happened to have created our policies to kick out

> **There is not enough money on the planet to save a community without fathers**

the fathers and keep the mothers. Virtually every social program, whether it's Juvenile Justice, Boys and Girls Clubs, Head Start or Charter Schools, is an attempt to fill the social and psychological gaps left by a lack of fathers, in particular, and by a lack of male role models in general, in certain communities.

The good news: teen pregnancies are down. The bad news: not enough has changed. The children in welfare communities remain unacceptably poor, trapped by inner-city crime and unprepared schools.

The American Dream is built on a tripod of three legs: strong families, quality education and hard work. What we did in the War On Poverty was to turn all three of them on their heads. We created incentives to break up families, so that now in the inner cities 80 percent of the Black kids literally grow up with only one parent from birth to age 18. We then followed that by this unbelievably perverse attitude in the inner-city Black community that if you do your studies, get high grades and pay attention to the teacher, you're acting white. And as Bill Cosby asked so famously: "Then what's acting Black?" Well, the answer is, if acting White means getting good grades in school, then maybe everybody ought to be acting White. I don't know why it should be acting White. It should be acting White, Green, Black, Yellow, Red or Purple. In other words, it should be acting intelligently as an Adult. That's why this book is *Adults Only*. We compromised the Work Ethic by offering welfare for life. No job, just checks. Well, in 1998 we changed all that around.

> The American Dream is built on a tripod of three legs: strong families, quality education and hard work

There were people who had not worked for generations. For them, getting a job was like literally being a fish out of water.

There are truly heroic role models in our inner-cities. People like my friend Carlton who teaches kids in the inner-city how to use computers. People like my friend Malachi who teaches inner-city kids how to play golf and, most importantly, my friend Amefika who started the first charter school in Palm Beach County. I was at his retirement dinner in 2006. A few people made speeches. Two of them come to mind. The first was his son Diriki, who is now a high school student. Dereki said that the most extraordinary thing about going to a charter school with his dad as a headmaster is that you share your dad with a hundred other boys who don't have fathers. When he said that, there was not a dry eye in the house.

The second speech was mine. I was the only White person there. I said that the Black community waiting around for some sort of financial payback for the untold misery of centuries gone by is the equivalent to saying, "Voting is for old people." Because while they're waiting, they're living in substandard houses, they have high crime, low-end jobs, shorter life expectancies, drugs and many other negative aspects of American life.

So by now you're saying, "Ok, Sid, give us your answer. Tell us how term-limited Congressmen and balanced budgets will revive families in the inner-city." Well, you're going to be disappointed. I'm stuck, and I've been working on this for a really long, long time. Term limited Congressmen will be able to have an *Adults Only* discussion, saying things you're not allowed to say out loud. A balanced budget would put huge pressure on social program spending. There is no obvious legislative solution to a *crisis of values*. But there is a direction for hope. The Black community is the only subset in America with an unelected national leadership. If you think of the Jewish community, the Hispanic community, the Catholic community, think of any subset and ask, "Who's their leader?" It's very hard to come up with somebody. You may come up with a prominent person from that ethnic group, but nobody would say that Joe Lieberman is the leader of the Jewish community, and nobody would say Marco Rubio is the leader of the Hispanic community. Most people would say that Jesse Jackson, and maybe to a lesser degree, Al Sharpton, are the leaders of Black community, and can in fact turn millions of votes in one direction or another.

When the leader of the Black community was Martin Luther King, who was working to get the Black community to join the opportunity society, everything was possible. The statement that resonates to this day is the dream of America where you were "judged by the content of your character and not by the color of your skin." But when leadership became Jesse Jackson and Al Sharpton and their victimization and reparations philosophy, everything became impossible. It doesn't matter whether their stands on these issues are persuasive or correct. It only matters that waiting forever to get payback is very destructive to an entire ethnic group.

Even if the checks came, two generations of not demanding the strongest families, the best education and the greatest work ethic have weakened the entire community. So the hope is as follows: The Black community will update its leadership. A young Bill Cosby, high standards, straight talking, *Adults Only* Black leader will emerge to demand that the Black community strive to reach its potential, and become a full participant in our affluent society and have a fair shot at the American Dream.

A huge national challenge burdened by the failed family structure is America's Educational System.

Education

The Achilles Heel of America

The Education Iron Law of Adults Only is: *A school is as good as the parents of the students.* It's true all the time. For all of you bragging about having great schools in Bergen County, New Jersey; Montgomery County, Maryland; Nassau and Suffolk Counties, New York; or Marin County, California, pat yourselves on the back. It's not your schools, principals, students or teachers. It's *you*. You are the entire reason little Johnny is going to grow up to earn his Harvard Law Degree. Take your same buildings, principals and teachers and put them in Central City Detroit, Chicago or Cleveland and what do you have? Continued disappointment, high dropout rates, ongoing disciplinary problems and graduates who can't read their own diplomas.

Pure and simple. We haven't figured it out. We are great at educating little geniuses and disasters at educating at-risk, single-parent kids, the ones who really need it. We are a country whose jobs are smarter than its students. That's why the wage gap keeps growing.

Let's explore two concepts that can make real changes in educating at-risk students. These two "magic bullets" are:

- PHONICS
- CHARTER SCHOOLS

We will never totally make up for fatherless communities and poor leadership, but we can make inroads. Let's start with the basics, reading. Most of you had the same reading teacher... Mom. Mom continually prompted you with those three special words, "Sound it out! Sound it out! Sound it out!" Yes, you were phonics literate by the age of six. Being phonics literate is like riding a bicycle... you only have to learn it once. Not all kids learn from Mom. Some Moms have poor literacy skills. Some have too many kids, no husband and not enough time. Some houses don't have enough books. What then?

> **There is no obvious legislative solution to a crisis in values**

We wait for the kids to reach school age expecting the teacher to show them how to read. Not so fast. You see, many schools teach Whole Language, a modern form of hieroglyphics, or word recognition. In other words, these youngsters are taught to recognize the letter combinations, but not to sound them out. After you learn "cat" you have to start all over to learn "bat" and again to learn "hat." These youngsters learn to memorize... not read. Mom's kids can read almost 3,000 words after first grade. Teacher's kids can read only 400 hundred. If you don't believe me ask a teacher over 50. By the way, there's a villain in this story... the text book publishers. There's great money for them in eight-year reading programs, but not in *Peter Pan* and *Alice in Wonderland*.

Every Charter School teaches Phonics. They have to. Charter Schools are the unsung heroes of American education... gifts to parents and guardians watching their hopes and dreams fade with their child's stubborn illiteracy. Every charitable and government sponsored program directed at inner city kids has one objective: to make up for the missing father. Nothing comes closer than Charter Schools. Charter Schools are community-based and publicly funded, but only loosely controlled by the central school district. In real life, Charter Schools are inner-city educational incubators using too little money, with inadequate facilities, often run by a strong Black male role model for a bunch of young, at-risk students who are not succeeding in the public school system. Charter Schools have the *biggest* problems and the *smallest* budgets. They are allotted as little as one-third the total per-pupil spending that is allotted for district schools. Charter Schools have inexperienced teachers, out-of-date, often rented buildings and little district administrative support. Indeed, at times the school district administration is openly hostile to these breakaway mavericks. And yet, Charter Schools may save American public education as we know it, because public schools and Charter Schools are in different businesses. Public schools are in the education business. Charter Schools are in the life-saving business.

They're not the same. Public school teachers in the inner city are putting in their three years, waiting for tenure and a ticket to the suburbs. Indeed, of all the teachers who both

A school is as good as the parents of the students

live and work in the inner cities, 40 percent send their kids to private schools. The Charter School teacher is answering a calling and committing to an extended period of teaching children three levels of respect: for self; for peers; and for authority. Public schools get a mix of prepared children, from the <u>eve</u>ready to the <u>never</u>eady. Charter Schools take the nevereadies and perform miracles. Virtually all Charter School children are former public school failures.

When we talk about Charter School lives, you probably think we're talking about the students themselves. Well, we are, along with the teachers, the staff and the community at large.

VIOLENT CRIMES IN CHARTER SCHOOLS ARE ONE FOURTH OF VIOLENT CRIMES IN PUBLIC SCHOOLS. At least, that's true in Philadelphia... a city truly with mean streets. In other words, Charter School kids, those public school failures, become authority-respecting, literate youngsters striving for a quality life in America. If my suspicions are correct (somebody please do the study...fast), violent crimes by young inner-city Black boys would be dramatically reduced OUTSIDE the schools, as well as inside, if we would just support Charter Schools enough to enable them to grow bigger, faster. There is a 75 percent reduction in in-school violent crime from arson to rape. The life you save may be mine—or yours—or, more likely, a student's or teacher's. This Adults Only approach to education reform is a true lifesaver for the community at large.

> We are a country whose jobs are smarter than its students

Republicans might have to give up the dream of universal vouchers. Democrats may have to give up the dream of no reform. But Americans could get the fabulous result of turning the nevereadies into the evereadies. The lives we save will literally be our own.

Other needed educational reforms worth mentioning include:

• Combat pay for selected inner-city teachers

• Variable pay by subject to attract teachers from all disciplines

• Honest reporting of costs to include both capital and
  operating expenditures

Believe me, we better make it work. At-risk kids not saved by new Black leadership or school reform will too often wind up in our criminal justice system, where the trick is to keep them there.

Crime

Stick 'Em Up

*E*verything discussed in the last two chapters is on display at your local prison. Take the tour. First, you realize that our prisons are "home" to way more men than women. Next, you see a disproportionate share of minorities (Black males are six times more likely to commit violent crimes than White males). There are as many young Black males in prison as in college. You have to look closer still to find the next two attributes. Prisoners have no fathers about 70 percent of the time, an alarming, though hardly new, number. That's a rate about double the general population. Next, prisoners can't read. Twenty percent are totally illiterate, and a great many more are functionally illiterate. In other words, take a fatherless, young Black male early dropout, and it's likely there's a jail cell with his name on it. That's why the last two chapters were so important. New leadership, Charter Schools, all the social interventions for at-risk kids better work, because once they go over the crime line, we're all in trouble.

The single most important fact about crime is: *THERE IS NO SUCH THING AS A FIRST OFFENDER.*

Spend a day at your local lockup. Every time (not some or most of the time, *every* time) an officer brings in a new arrestee... check the screen. There in bright, Microsoft letters are his "priors." What do you see? You see that 100 percent of these arrestees have already been arrested, tried and convicted of other crimes. How do you think we got their mug shots? We took those pictures when they were being booked for earlier crimes. By now you're asking. "Why did we let them out?" Exactly! We didn't keep them because our justice system refuses to accept that *there is no such thing as a first offender*. In other words, the violent crime with the seven-year sentence became the second... or third... or fourth... or fifth chance opportunity with an 18-month sentence. Well, guess what? Between the 18 months and the seven years, we can only guess how many crimes that felon committed. Remember, we only see the ones that got caught. Everybody has to make a living. Those guys are in the thuggery business. I want them in the off-the-streets business. The day they cross the crime line, we need to shift our gears from saving *them* to saving *ourselves*. That means more time in more jails, resulting in less crime and a healthier community.

There is no such thing as a first offender

Communities that increase time decrease crime

Then there's that "Recidivism" rate. Everyone needs to learn the word RECIDIVISM, which means, "We let them out and they commit more crimes"... as often as 70 percent of the time. Again, those are only the ones we caught. As far as the other 30 percent are concerned, if we knew who they were at sentencing, we could adjust. But we don't. So instead of *punishing* all of America by letting everyone out early, let's *reward* all of America by keeping the felons locked up as long as possible. The life you save may be mine – or yours. *Communities that increase time decrease crime.* Those communities that think you decrease crime by building Youth Centers soon learn that felons think "shooting" and "scoring" are drug words, not basketball accomplishments.

Immigration

Hola! Neighbor

My wife, Esther, is very blessed, (and not just because she married me). When Esther, her brother and her parents escaped from Communist Poland in 1958, they landed in Brooklyn, New York. There were no English-as-a-Second-Language classes for Polish immigrants to languish in while not learning English. There were no government checks available to make not working an option. And there were no Sanctuary Cities to make law breaking less risky. Esther and her brother are living high-quality American lives with their respective families. Their parents, no longer with us, got to enjoy citizenship, home ownership and grand-children..."nachas" as the Jewish Community would say... another happy American Dream ending.

We think we're having a debate about immigration in this country. We're not. I know we're not because I'm the only one asking the whereabouts of the new Swedes, Poles, Russians, Indians, Chinese, Spaniards and scores of other nationalities that have made our country so colorful and so great. Today, people call themselves pro-immigration and call for more Mexicans, Latin Americans and Spanish- speaking opportunities. Believe me, if you're not as concerned about those other continents (Asia, Europe, Africa and Australia) as you are about Central and South America, you are many things, but pro-Immigration is not one of them. To me, if we don't have enough people to fill our ever-growing number of jobs, we need to increase our annual *LEGAL* immigration quotas from around the world. That's *PRO*-immigration. Saying that those who cut the line should be ahead of those who waited patiently is *anti*-immigration and frankly, insulting to the vast majority of the world's nationalities who hope someday to share in our great fortune.

The debate we didn't have would have been about global immigration and America's needs. The debate we are having is about a disproportionate amount of one ethnic group... Hispanic... entering our country legally and illegally, and initiating a call for the end of assimilation as we know it. America is scared, scared that one day we will become Canada. We are scared that the hole in Canada's heart known as Quebec will be replicated by something called Mexifornia, a hole in America's heart. There are many key foundation blocks that have given America its very blessed 230+ years. Assimilation is one of them.

My very specific, comprehensive immigration proposal, in my opinion, is workable, humane and respectful of all special groups, including the largest...Americans.

English shall become the "official" language of the United States. This is one of the three key Constitutional Amendments I strongly recommend if America wants a 21st century at least as good as its 20th. It should not have come to this. There are more Americans of German descent than any other. Nobody is suggesting we vote in German. As our official language, English will have a monopoly on voting and Citizenship Tests. This is not about private signs in Chinatown or the kosher butcher's Hebrew sign. This is about our nation's business... voting. We must restore our "e pluribus unum" voting system.

Our borders must be secure. It seems silly to even have to say it. America has a front door. Everyone needs to use it. Those who say we don't let enough people in, consider this: If we let everyone in who wanted to come, we would be a different, and much poorer, country. Also, America has more legal immigrants every year than the rest of the world combined. All policies are possible with protected borders. No policy is enforceable with sieves for security. Indeed, when people who wish us harm come to our country, we are all at risk. 9/11 was an Equal Opportunity slaughter. We were all targeted regardless of race, religion or immigration status.

No policy is enforceable with sieves for borders

ID cards are not just feasible, they're essential. Every non-citizen should have an electronic, bar-coded, holograph encoded ID card. Period. If you're here and you're not a citizen (yet), we need to know it. However, if you plan to start a new life here, the day you get *your* card, the clock starts ticking on *your* Citizenship Application. We've been debating immigration for 25 years. Shame on us for being no closer to having these non-citizen ID cards now than we were then. Term Limits, where are you?

The above three recommendations create a feasible, rational immigration policy for our country. What they don't do is deal with the immigration "burro in the living room," or, as we all know them, the *12 Million*. Remember, there are an estimated 12 million illegal immigrants in America. Some snuck in. Some were let in temporarily, but never left. No recommended immigration policy is serious without specific credible answers to the *"12 MILLION PEOPLE PROBLEM." We're not kicking them out*. That doesn't mean they belong here or deserve to be here. That only means that the America

I know is the most tolerant and benevolent nation on the planet. We don't fight fire with fire. And we don't seek an eye for an eye. Our justice has mercy.

Not only do they get to stay, but *their kids get to go to our schools* (K-12). They will enjoy the protection of our policemen, firefighters, military and courts. They get to remain with dignity.

Opportunity is the biggest benefit, and they may (must) seek opportunity. They are expected to work on the books for at least the minimum wage with the same payroll and income withholding taxes as everyone else. Their Social Security contributions are recorded in case they are citizens when they are old enough to collect. With opportunity goes dignity. America's strength is in treating everyone with dignity. The *12 Million* will be no exception.

There is no public charity. We gave schools, opportunities and employment. We will not offer Social Security, Medicare, Medicaid, Food Stamps or publicly financed healthcare. Private non-profits and civic groups may do as they please. Those that came for benefits will leave. Those that came for opportunity will stay. It's their choice. No coercion is involved. The beauty of assimilation is that it is self selecting. At the same time there are no fines for "breaking in," just a requirement that the Rule of Law will reassert itself into the lives of the *12 Million*.

If there are criminals within the 12 Million, they will do their time before deportation, but deported they will be. We're not kicking anyone out, except those who literally bite the hands that feed them.

The road to citizenship starts the day they sign up for their ID card. That is Day 1. The Bangladeshi who went to the American Embassy the day before will always be ahead of them. Our per-nation quotas will not be modified to either accommodate or hurt the

12 Million. They'll just have to wait until their date comes up… the date after all the other global applicants who followed the rules. Our annual legal immigration quota is just over 500,000. It could grow if we had labor shortages. Having the *12 Million* in our country makes that very unlikely.

Over time, with secure borders and successful ID cards, the *12 Million* will become less. Some will become citizens. Some will leave voluntarily. Most will work and wait.

There are non-legislative attitudes that must become prevalent if America is to have another great century. We are the "e pluribus unums." This entire book has not one, hyphenated American (except in this paragraph). No African-Americans. No Mexican-Americans. No Italian-Americans. You get the point. We're all Americans…

The beauty of Assimilation is that it is self selecting

plain and simple. We may agree or disagree. We can walk a picket line or march on Washington, but *if anyone is interested in joining this great nation, they need to plan on loving it* as much as I do – or plan on going somewhere else. There are 200 other choices.

The reality of today's world is that unprotected borders or casual vigilance creates a risk for any country, not the least of which is the threat of Terrorism.

It's The War, Stupid

*E*verything has a Foreign Policy component. It's time to take a meandering walk through policies involving foreign relations, farms and energy. We will visit America's Heartland, tundra, prairie, tar sands, Gulf Coast, and, of course, the Capitol, seesawing from cynicism to optimism, and from selfishness to patriotism.

Everybody in Washington puts America second

Know this: We will not win the War on Terrorism without Term Limits and a Balanced Budget Amendment. That's right. We have lost before we have fought. Not in Baghdad, or Kabul, or Teheran, but in Washington, D.C., where we are currently structured to guarantee our loss in this or just about any other war.

Everybody in Washington puts America second. That's sad. If you are a lobbyist, your fees come before your country. I assume you are both patriotic and product loyal. But I am equally sure that when your lobbying and your patriotism come into conflict, it's the patriotism that gets tossed overboard. If you are a Congressman or Senator, your reelection comes before your country. The days of Henry Clay's, "I would rather be right than President," are long gone. When your reelection requires taking bundled contributions from those same conflicted lobbyists, your patriotism becomes tied to theirs. When they throw their patriotism over the side, they throw yours over with it. Before we all start feeling morally superior to those Washingtonians, we need to look at our own lobbyists… from left to right, from teachers to tobacco, from Planned Parenthood to petroleum products, and for every interest group in between. How many of us would send our own lobbyists home to save our country? Let's find out.

First, let's define the War on Terrorism. If you believe that there are legions of bad guys, generally defined by a militant belief in Islamic fundamentalism, then you understand the War on Terrorism.

We will not win the War on Terrorism without Term Limits and a Balanced Budget Amendment

You do not have to believe that specific strategies or theaters are essential to the War. There are no litmus tests. You do not have to sign on to Iraq, Afghanistan, Iran or any subset of this War. If you think the world is sunny and that 9/11 was an aberration, and that the world would leave us alone if we left the world alone, then think again. The *Adults Only* objective for the War on Terrorism is simple: We Win, They Lose. Yes, I know I shamelessly borrowed that phrase from Ronald Reagan's prescription for the Cold War. Some things are hard to improve on. At least I give credit. Yes, we win, they lose. Without

Term Limits and a Balanced Budget Amendment, We Can't Win and They Can't Lose. Let's connect the dots.

The good news about the Terrorists is that they're a one product operation…Oil. No oil, no money. No money… no weapons, no recruits, no training, no media. In short, no money… no war. We Win, They Lose. Yet here we are years after 9/11, and we have dealt with the Terrorism threat by *DOUBLING* oil prices. Yes, *WE* continue to finance the Terrorists, who continue to kill *our* soldiers with *our* oil money that winds up in *their* hands. The finger points right at Washington… at those Congressmen and Senators who are unwilling to shun the lobbyists who fund their campaigns in exchange for the votes, which have the unintended consequences of funding our enemies. We could take the Surrender approach, give up our cars, significantly reduce our collective standard of living, and hopefully impress (certainly not scare) our enemies into declaring victory and leaving us alone. But this is an *Adults Only* philosophy. I have a better idea. If we had Term Limits and a Balanced Budget Amendment, we would be the world's Number 1 energy PRODUCER to match up with our long-term status as the world's Number 1 energy CONSUMER. How easy is that? Surprisingly easy. We can, in short order, create an energy armada built on everything we know and some things we'll learn. We need domestic oil, natural gas, coal, shale, tar sands, wind, biofuels, nuclear, solar, ocean tides, batteries, fuel cells and hydrogen. I can't list more, because I don't know them or they haven't been invented yet. The day we commit to all of these technologies is the day the Terrorists start losing, squeezed by shrinking revenues and hungry followers. There isn't an energy source I mentioned that requires government subsidies. Some require continued private investment, but there's no shortage of that money. Ask Ford and General Motors. However, there is a shortage of permission… permission from elected bodies at all levels, federal, state and local… to turn American ingenuity loose. There is no shortage of lobbyists whose very jobs (and fees) depend on stopping our energy independence.

Stopping our energy independence means keeping the price of oil high and the Terrorists armed. I strongly suggest that we disturb the Alaskan Caribou and the Florida sharks with our oil wells. We should threaten some views with wind farms, compromise our air with coal-fired furnaces and bother our esthetics with solar panels. You get the idea. We Adults will do almost anything to make America strong and the Terrorists poor. And before you tar and feather me for showing no reverence for pristine air and global warming, make sure you know my side: *THEY'RE TRYING TO KILL US!* I'm not against clean air, smog- free Los Angeles or nuclear-free neighborhoods. It's just that I'M FOR LIVING! *They're* for killing us. When we are the world's energy Superstore with oil prices cut to ribbons and Terrorists cut to shreds, we can go back to the polite lobbyist-financed arguments about which fuels make the best long-term sense for that delicate balance of improving standards of living and cleaning up the planet. But for *now*, Saving Lives is Job 1.

Good news! The future of energy rides on Route 66, right through America's Heartland. It's too soon to tell, but biofuel could make oil look like a drop in the bucket. We could "grow" untold gallons of gas, reap the harvest and do it all over again next year. It could be the mother lode. Of course, we know better. We know that a Federal Government without Term Limits or a Balanced Budget Amendment has built-in incentives to keep us from becoming a biomass behemoth. Rewind. Once upon a time, in 1932, our farmers suffered through terribly adverse conditions. A drought had turned our Heartland into a dustbowl. The dustbowl couldn't feed the farmer's family, much less all of America. America was both scared and generous... scared that too many farmers would descend upon our cities looking for jobs that were lost in the Depression... and so generous that a complex federal program of farm subsidies and guarantees would allow them to keep their land and rebuild their businesses. Fast forward. Here we are 75 years later. Our "emergency" farm program has seen hundreds of billions of dollars of federal aid in many forms... subsidies, loan guarantees, import restrictions, payments for not planting, government purchases of crop over-supplies and guaranteed minimum prices. Examples include federal guarantees on loans to *TOBACCO* farmers and restrictions on importing sugar from our Caribbean friends, leaving Americans to pay twice the world price for our sugar. Eighty percent of all farm subsidies go to large Agribusiness corporations. Then there's ethanol. American ethanol is corn based. That means it takes seven gallons of fuel to produce eight gallons of corn based ethanol. That's not an energy program. That's a corporate welfare program. There are too many lobbyists who want to keep it that way. Brazil's ethanol program is sugar-cane based. It works. Less fuel in. More fuel out. The obvious question is, "Why don't we use sugar-cane based ethanol?" You already know the answer. It's because our Congressmen and Senators-for-life with the unlimited budgets want to continue restricting sugar-cane imports so that Americans can continue to pay our domestic sugar-cane growers twice the world price... sugar cane at twice the world price is not the answer to our energy problems, which means that the Terrorists continue to kill us, the Congressmen continue to get their unlimited campaign contributions and our $45 trillion unfunded liabilities continue to grow at a rate of $1.1 billion per day. Farm subsidies are $25 billion per year, adding almost $70 million per day to our children's debt. Added bonuses include this huge corporate welfare program that no other industry has access to, good farmland wasted on inefficient plantings (like tobacco), and, most of all, no way to tell which biofuel is efficient and appealing to America's energy consumers. Until we know that, the Terrorists will win. Once we know that, the Terrorists are cooked... or boiled in oil, as I like to say.

I have a dream (thank you, Dr. King). I dream that one day (very soon), all American farmers will get together and, in one loud patriotic voice, yell, "Thank you, America. Thank you for 75 years of support. We can go it alone from here." Farmers love America. But do they love their subsidies more?

There you have it. Energy, farm and war policies...all made worse by Congressmen seeking a lifetime gig with unlimited blank checks. Terrorism is about more than money. It's about life and death… yours and mine.

Until "We the children" becomes "We the people" once again, America will be "We the terrorized."

Pollution

Cleaning Up Our Act

POOR COUNTRIES ARE DIRTY COUNTRIES. It's not that they have different values or goals. It's just that they have no money. Curing an unhealthy environment, from the neighborhood lot to the ozone layer, always requires the same antidote... money.

In the mid-19th century, America had a 15-year string of double-digit growth. Boy, did we pollute! The Industrial Revolution roared in, and trains, boats and factories belched out the blackest smoke imaginable. Our rivers were repositories for all kinds of industrial and animal waste. Our environmental consciousness was sagging, to say the least. More than 100 years later, following one Civil and two World Wars, we decided to clean up our country. From Boston Harbor to the Hudson River, from Pittsburgh to Los Angeles, from coal scrubbers to catalytic converters, from landfills to recycling bins... America found religion. And that's a good thing. We're a happier and prouder nation. Why now and why not then? Money. It took more than 100 years of an Industrial Revolution for America to feel rich enough to impose the taxes, voluntary and statutory, that financed the fight against pollution of all kinds.

The world remains a very dirty place. The now defunct Soviet Union became famous for its Black Forests of Eastern Europe. The "new" Russia is an infant, struggling to feed and employ its people, leaving little time or money for a consciousness raising cleanup. India and China are in the early stages of their Industrial Revolutions. They have almost two-and-one-half-billion people between them,

Poor countries are dirty countries

more than half literally dirt poor. When elections come, they don't vote for the "cleanest" candidate. They vote for the "growingest" candidate. America didn't outlaw pollution-belching factories. We just exported them. In Argentina, the poor neighborhoods are litter infested. In Haiti the concept of sewers is still being learned. In Indonesia, the world's fourth most populous nation, people think that trees are a primary energy source. So they cut them down.

Globally, over two-and-a-half billion people lack electricity. Who's going to tell them they can't have it? Not me. I'm also not going to tell Americans to get rid of their

Rich countries are clean countries

SUV's… or Saudis to sell their yachts. The thought that people should embrace a lower standard of living going forward is simply not going to happen. We're keeping *our* houses and cars, and the developing nations can't wait until they get *theirs*. We can pretend all we want that high-minded low-wage people want to save the world before they provide for their families, but we know it's not true. We also know this... almost every speech about shared sacrifices is made by someone who just got off a private jet. No complaints here.

As Adults, the solution to Cleaning Up Our Act, globally, becomes obvious. *Just as Poor Countries Are Dirty Countries... Rich Countries Are Clean Countries.* We will have a cleaner planet as we become a wealthier planet. Those without electricity will always use trees for cooking. Those with electricity can build their villages into communities, and then into cities. Preaching sacrifice to the poor is hypocrisy. Exporting moral superiority is insulting. The fastest way to a pristine planet is by making the world wealthy... the whole world. All remaining pockets of poverty will remain purveyors of pollution. The newly affluent will tax themselves to improve their own environment.

> **The fastest way to a pristine planet is by making the world wealthy**

The best policies America can adopt toward the developing world are wealth-creating ones... free trade, the Rule of Law, contracts, private property, competition and an independent judiciary. The faster they grow and the richer they get, the more willing and able they will be to raise the bar on cleanliness standards.

The two biggest global issues are terrorism and pollution. Fighting terrorism requires the realization that people want to live. Fighting pollution requires the realization that people want to live *BETTER.*

Conclusion

Call To Action

EMOCRACY IS NOT A SPECTATOR SPORT. It has become one. We turned our government over to our elected officials only to realize that they won't give it back. Most parents have had that argument with their (usually) teenaged children. We gave them everything and they can't show their appreciation. So it is in Washington. We gave them a lifestyle they could never dream of, and they are incapable of showing their appreciation.

Of course it's not about civility and appreciation. It's about prosperity and security for our children… and the possibility that we may have already traded them away. We do not know which bump in the road the fiscal can will hit. We are only certain that it is there, lying in wait. It could be next week, next year or next decade. It could come out of a housing crisis through failing banks or a stock market reaction. A failure by a major financial institution could be a disaster. OPEC switching out of the Dollar and into the Euro could be financially catastrophic. Same with China. Downgrading of certain government or corporate bonds would be a major hit. I'm not a gloom-and-doomer. I'm a concerned American, father and grandfather.

Fortunately, our Founding Fathers were smarter than all of us. The rules of our game, the United States Constitution, still enable us to make significant changes in a short amount of time. This leads to our Call To Action.

OPEC switching out of the dollar and into the Euro could be financially catastrophic

Remember, our electees are not bad people. They're good people living with bad incentives. If they didn't have to pre-sell their votes... and earn their bundled campaign contributions that will keep them in Washington forever... the system would still be working. Our Call To Action is not for our Congressmen. It's for our citizens... you, me, our neighbors, our co-workers, our families and our co-congregants. I will not promise an easy road to the recovery of our birthright. I mostly promise hard work and countless unpaid volunteer hours required in keeping a Democratic Republic.

The fastest way to a pristine planet is by making the world wealthy

TO TAKE BACK OUR COUNTRY:

You've already answered the call by making it this far.

THE MISSION:

The *Adults Only* Trilogy of:

- TERM LIMITS

- BALANCED BUDGETS

- ENGLISH as our OFFICIAL LANGUAGE

THE TACTIC:

- PROMOTE THE PLEDGE

Every voter in America gets to elect a Congressman every two years. In half of these elections, every four years, we also vote for a President. In one third of these elections, we vote for a Senator.

IT'S YOUR JOB to make them take the PLEDGE:

Representative Candidate

I, _____, Candidate for Congressional District _____, State of _____, affirm that upon my election I will fully support the Adults Only Trilogy of United States Constitutional Amendments, which includes:

Term Limits

Balanced Budgets

English as our Official Language

I further understand that should I renege on this commitment, I will expect to be subject to Recall or diminished support in subsequent elections.

Senatorial Candidate

I, _____, Candidate for United States Senator from the State of _____, affirm that upon my election I will fully support the Adults Only Trilogy of United States Constitutional Amendments, which includes:

Term Limits

Balanced Budgets

English as our Official Language

I further understand that should I renege on this commitment, I will expect to be subject to Recall or diminished support in subsequent elections.

Presidential Candidate

I, _____, Candidate for President of the United States, affirm that, upon my election I will initiate the Adults Only trilogy of United States Constitutional Amendments, which includes:

Term Limits

Balanced Budgets

English as our Official Language

IT'S YOUR JOB to join with your take-back-the-government grass-roots neighbors and present the PLEDGE to your federal candidates.

IT'S YOUR JOB to take the signed and unsigned PLEDGES to your community at large...every civic, religious, business, academic and political group in your district.

IT'S YOUR JOB to take the signed and unsigned PLEDGES to every newspaper reporter, TV news journalist, local magazine newsletter, blogger and letters-to-the-editor gatekeeper.

IT'S YOUR JOB to make the PLEDGE the Number 1 issue at the next election...at every forum, debate and town-hall meeting.

IT'S THE CANDIDATES' JOB to sign the PLEDGE, or risk the consequences.

IT'S MY JOB to Thank You for all that you have done, to Thank You for all that you are doing and, mostly, to Thank You for all that you are about to do.

It's not just your country. It's not just my country. It's everyone's country. If enough "everyones" fight for our country, we will keep it. If not enough do, we won't.

Sid Dinerstein
Advocate for Good Government

The United States Constitution

Condensed

The Constitution of the United States was written after the Revolutionary War, which gave people in America freedom from Britain. The people were ready to become a nation and considered themselves Americans. But they objected to a national government out of fear they would be under the same laws that prevailed under British rule. They had just won their independence and didn't want to give it away to a national government.

George Washington felt that the states would not survive alone, and that the country needed to be united. The Articles of Confederation was the first plan of government. It formed a republic, which elected representatives to run the country, although many thought one person, such as George Washington, should be that person.

The country did not work well under this new plan. There were many problems that caused the representatives to take a closer look at the plan. The states that were once afraid of a strong government now had a weak one that couldn't function effectively.

The states began to argue over borders, trade, money and taxes. These arguments led to a convention in 1786. Only five of the 13 representatives attended, but they agreed that the Articles needed to be changed. Secret meetings began, and the Preamble was written to form a better plan of government, to provide peace and justice, to defend the nation against its enemies and to promote the well-being of the country.

The Preamble

We the people of the United States, in Order to form a more perfect Union, establish Justice, insure domestic Tranquillity, provide for the common defense, promote the general Welfare, and secure the Blessings of Liberty to ourselves and our Posterity, do ordain and establish this Constitution for the United States of America.

Articles of the Constitution

Article 1

States that Congress has control over legislation, and that the Congress be divided into two parts, or chambers: the House of Representatives and the Senate.

The House of Representatives

- *Elected by the people to two year terms*
- *Must be 25 years old*
- *Must be citizen of the U.S.*
- *Must live in the state where elected*

The Senate

- *Each state has two senators*
- *Senators serve six year terms*
- *One-third of senators are elected at a time*
- *Must be at least 30 years old*
- *Must be a citizen of the U.S. at least nine years*
- *Must live in the state where elected*
- *The vice president presides over the Senate, only can cast a vote in the event of a tie*
- *In his absence, the president pro tempore presides*
- *After the House has voted to impeach an elected official the Senate tries the case. Favorable votes by two-thirds of the of the Senate are required to convict*
- *Tax bills originate in the House. After a bill passes the House and the Senate, it goes before the president, who has 10 days to sign it or veto it. If the president does nothing, the bill becomes law automatically*

The Congress

- *Collects taxes*
- *Regulates commerce*
- *Coins money*
- *Manage a postal system*
- *Declares war*
- *Creates a Judicial system*
- *Maintains a military*
- *Make laws necessary for carrying out the Constitution*
- *Made it illegal to arrest and jail citizens*
- *Determines all monetary spending by the government*

Article 2

Executive power vested in the president of the United States of America

- *Ensures that the nation's laws are carried out and enforced*
- *Serves a four year term*
- *Formally elected by the members of the Electoral College*
- *Must be 35 years old*
- *Must be a United States citizen, born in the United States*
- *Must have been a resident of the country for at least 14 years*
- *In case of death of the president, the vice president becomes president*
- *Has wide authority in the Executive Branch*
- *Serves as commander in chief of the Armed Forces*
- *Has power to grant pardons in criminal cases*
- *Has supervisory responsibility in the Executive Branch departments*
- *The president, vice president and other top officials can be removed from office if they commit serious offenses*

Article 3
Judicial Power of the United States
- *Judicial power is vested in the Supreme Court*
- *Supreme Court has some control over the legal system*
- *Supreme Court justices hold their seat for life, unless they violate significant laws*
- *Grants Americans the right to a jury trial*
- *Requires the trial be held in the state in which the crime was allegedly committed*
- *Allows   Allows conviction for treson only if there are two witnesses to the crime, or if the accused person confesses in court*

Article 4
Full Faith and Credit
- *States must accept most laws and legal decisions made by other states*
- *States must offer most fundamental legal rights to both nonresidents and residents of the state*
- *Perpetrators of serious crimes may not take refuge in other states*
- *Congress controls the admission of new states*
- *The Federal government may use federal buildings, land, and property in any way it chooses*
- *The Federal government obligates itself to protect the states and to intervenep in domestic problems if needed*

Article 5
Proposing Amendments
- *States may propose an Amendment if, two-thirds of the statess call a constitutional convention. Passage requires favorable votes by three-quarters of the states*
- *Congress may propose an Amendment if two-thirds of the members in both chambers vote to support it Passage requires favorable votes by three-quarters of the state legislatures*
- *After Congress proposes the Amendment, it takes three-quarters of the state legislatures to approve it.*

Article 6

The Laws of the United States
  - *All laws made–federal, state or local, must conform to the laws set forth in the Constitution*
  - *All judges must hold the Constitution above any other law*
  - *All member of Congress, state legislatures, state and federal judges, and state and federal executive officials must agree to support the Constitution*

Article 7

Ratification of the Conventions
  - *Only nine of the original 13 were needed to approve the Constitution*

Bill of Rights

The first 10 Amendments were put into effect (ratified) on December 13, 1791. They form the Bill of Rights.

Amendment 1
- *Guarantees freedom of religion, freedom of speech, freedom of the press and freedom of association and assemble*
- *Guarantees freedom to demand a change in government policies*

Amendment 2
- *Grants the right to bear arms*

Amendment 3
- *Forbids the housing of soldiers in people's homes during peacetime without their permission and allows such housing during wartime only according to law*

Amendment 4
- *Forbids police and other government officials from searching people's homes or officesfrom seizing their property without reasonable grounds to believe a crime has been committed*
- *Prohibits search unless a search warrant is obtained from a judge*

Amendment 5
There are five important protections in the Fifth Amendment.
- *No one may be punished for a crime unless he or she has been found guilty in a court of law. "Innocent until proven guilty."*
- *Double jeopardy-A person may be tried only once for the same crime*

- *A person may not be forced to testify against himself or herself in any criminal case. "Pleading the fifth."*
- *The government may not deprive anyone of life, liberty or property*
- *The government may not take any person's property unless it is necessary for the public or if the government pays a fair price for it*

Amendment 6

- *A person accused of a crime is entitled to a speedy and public trial*
- *A defendant is entitled to be tried in the area in which the crime was committed*
- *The government may not prosecute a person without informing him or her of the nature of the charges*
- *The accused has the right to cross-examination*
- *The accused has the right to subpoena witnesses to testify in court on his or her behalf*
- *The accused has the right to a lawyer for legal defense*

Amendment 7

- *The Seventh Amendment guarantees the right to a jury trial in some types of federal civil trials*

Amendment 8

- *A criminal defendant has the right to be released from jail before trial by posting a reasonable bail that will guarantee the defendent comes to trial*
- *The government may not impose unreasonable fines on convicted criminals*
- *The government may subject criminals to cruel and unusual punishment*

Amendment 9

- *The people retain an inalienable right whether or not it is specified in the Constitution*

Amendment 10

- *If a particular power was not assigned to the federal government by the Constitution, states may carry out that power unless otherwise forbidden by the Constitution*
- *People are free to act outside the scope of the federal government's powers*

Amendment 11

- *State governments have some immunity in federal courts*

Amendment 12

- *If no presidential candidate wins the majority of the Electoral College, the House of Representatives chooses the president and the Senate chooses the vice president*

Amendment 13

- *Slavery is illegal*

Amendment 14

- *Anyone born in the United States is a citizen and has the rights and liberties as granted in the Constitution*
- *States that bar men from voting will have their state's congressional record reduced significantly*
- *Persons loyal to the Confederacy in the Civil War could not serve in Congress unless two-thirds of Congress agreed to waive the restriction*
- *Civil War debts were declared uncollectable from the state and federal governments*

Amendments 15

- *People have the right to vote and cannot be stopped from doing so by the state or federal government because of race*

Amendment 16

- *Congress may impose an income tax*

Amendment 17

- *Each state elects two members to serve in the United States Senate. If there is a vacancy, the governor of that state may appoint someone to the position until an election can be held*

Amendment 18

- *Known as the "Prohibition Act," this Amendment bans alcohol. It was repealed in 1933*

Amendment 19

- *Women in the United States have the right to vote*

Amendment 20

- *The president and the vice president begin their terms of office on January 20 of each year following the presidential election*
- *Congressional sessions begin January 3*
- *In the event that a newly elected president dies before taking office, the newly elected vice president acts as president until a president is selected or until Congress chooses*
- *Congress has the ability to pass a law to determine the order of succession to the presidency after the vice president. The current succession: speaker of the House, president protem pore of the Senate, a sequence of cabinet members*

Amendment 21

- *This Amendment was ratified in 1933*
- *The Amendment grants each state the power to regulate alcohol in their respective states*

Amendment 22

- *A president may not serve more than two terms in office. This Amendment came as a response to Franklin D. Roosevelt's four terms*

Amendment 23

- *People living in Washington, D.C., may vote presidential elections*

Amendment 24

- *Citizens of the United States may be denied the right to vote based on failure to pay any poll or other tax*

Amendment 25

- *Ratified February 10, 1967*
- *If the president should resign for any reason, the vice president takes over the office*
- *If there is no vice president, the president can appoint a replacement with a majority approval from both houses of Congress*
- *If the president is unable to continue in office for any reason, the vice president will take over the office*
- *If the president seems unfit to fulfill his job as president, the Congress may strip him of his powers. He can regain his office by certifying that he is, in fact, fit. However, the president still may be declared unfit by the vice president and a two-thirds vote by each house of Congress*

Amendment 26

- *Citizens of the United States who are 18 years of age or older cannot be denied the right to vote*
- *Citizens must be at least 18 to vote*

Amendment 27

- *The rate of pay for members of Congress may not be changed until the House of Representatives election has occurred*

Introduction to the Declaration of Independence

From 1492, when Christopher Columbus raised the Spanish flag for King Ferdinand and Queen Isabella in the New World, a stream of explorers headed west out of Europe seeking a route to Asia and hoping to learn more about this new land. One of these was Amerigo Vespucci, after whom the name "America" was given to refer to the New World.

Europe began colonizing North America in the 16th century. The French established the first permanent European colony in St. Augustine, Florida; the Dutch established colonies in New Amsterdam, later to become New York City; and England's Queen Elizabeth I had Sir Walter Raleigh set up the first English colony of Virginia in 1585. The British went on to establish a total of 13 colonies in North America.

France relinquished all of its land east of the Mississippi River, except New Orleans, to England, after the French and Indian Wars. At the same time, the Spanish traded Florida to England for Cuba.

Taxation without representation became an issue in the colonies when the English Parliament passed the Stamp Act in March of 1765. For the first time in the 150-year history of the British colonies in America, Americans were required to pay taxes directly to England instead of to their own local legislatures. The colonies quickly united in opposition. Although the Stamp Act was repealed the following year, the English Parliament simultaneously passed the Declaratory Act stating that the British government had total power to legislate any laws governing the American colonies. Colonial opposition continued to mount against Britain.

England imposed more taxes on the colonies through the Townshend Revenue Acts of 1767. By 1768 colonists resisting taxation without representation began to unite in their actions against the British government.

On May 10, 1773, Britain's Tea Act took effect, imposing a three penny per pound import tax on tea arriving in the colonies. When colonists in Boston decided to send a shipment of tea back to England without paying any import duties, the royal governor of Massachusetts ordered harbor officials not to allow the ship to set sail until the tea taxes were paid. On the evening of December 16, 1773, a group of colonial activists disguised themselves as Mohawk Indians, boarded the ships, and proceeded to dump all 342 containers of tea into the harbor in what came to be known as "The Boston Tea Party."

England immediately initiated a series of coercive acts, called Intolerable Acts by Americans, shut down Boston Harbor until Massachusetts paid the taxes owed on the dumped tea, and placed Massachusetts under military rule. The colonists began to organize a intercolonial congress to overcome these coercive acts and discuss a common course of action against the British.

On September 5, 1774, the First Continental Congress met in Philadelphia. Among the 56 delegates, representing every colony except Georgia, were Patrick Henry, Georgia Washington, Sam Adams and John Hancock. They declared that the coercive acts were not to be obeyed and promoted the formation of local militia units. A Declaration and Resolves was adopted opposing all measures by the British that undermined self-rule. They asserted the rights of the colonists, including the rights to "life, liberty and property." In February 1775, a provincial congress took defensive preparations for war and England declared Massachusetts to be in a state of rebellion. On March 23, Patrick Henry delivered his famous "Give me liberty or give me death!" speech in Virginia. The conflict between Great Britain and the American colonies intensified.

On June 11, 1776, the Continental Congress appointed a committee consisting of Thomas Jefferson, Benjamin Franklin, John Adams, Roger Livingston and Roger Sherman to draft a declaration of independence. Jefferson was chosen by the committee to prepare the first draft of the declaration. He completed it in one day, and it was presented to the Congress with changes made by Adams and Franklin, on June 28. It was officially endorsed and adopted by the Continental Congress on July 4. The colonies banded together to break away from Britain's rule and declare themselves free and independent states. It's important to note that signers of the Declaration of Independence took an enormous risk with their lives. If Great Britain had managed to control the rebellion, each colonist who signed the document could have been tried, convicted and executed for treason against England.

The Declaration of Independence caused a Revolutionary War with Great Britain, which resulted in the establishment of a new nation–the United States of America.

Declaration of Independence

Action of Second Continental Congress, July 4, 1776

The unanimous Declaration of the thirteen
United States of America

(Colonists declared their independence from England
in a letter to King George III)

WHEN in the Course of human Events, it becomes necessary for one People to dissolve the Political Bands which have connected them with another, and to assume among the Powers of the Earth, the separate and equal Station to which the Laws of Nature and of Nature's God entitle them, a decent Respect to the Opinions of Mankind requires that they should declare the causes which impel them to the Separation.

WE hold these Truths to be self-evident, that all Men are created equal, that they are endowed by their Creator with certain unalienable Rights, that among these are Life, Liberty and the Pursuit of Happiness—That to secure these Rights, Governments are instituted among Men, deriving their just Powers from the Consent of the Governed, that whenever any Form of Government becomes destructive of these Ends, it is the Right of the People to alter or to abolish it, and to institute new Government, laying its Foundation on such Principles, and organizing its Powers in such Form, as to them shall seem most likely to effect their Safety and Happiness. Prudence, indeed, will dictate that Governments long established should not be changed for light and transient Causes; and accordingly all Experience hath shewn, that Mankind are more disposed to suffer, while Evils are sufferable, than to right themselves by abolishing the Forms to which they are accustomed. But when a long Train of Abuses and Usurpations, pursuing invariably the same Object, evinces a Design to reduce them under absolute Despotism, it is their Right, it is their Duty, to throw off such Government, and to provide new Guards for their future Security. Such has been the patient Sufferance of these Colonies; and such is now the Necessity which constrains them to alter their former Systems of Government. The History of the present King of Great-Britain is a History of repeated Injuries and Usurpations, all having in direct Object the Establishment of an absolute Tyranny over these States. To prove this, let Facts be submitted to a candid World. HE has refused his Assent to Laws, the most wholesome and necessary for the public Good. HE has forbidden his Governors to pass Laws of immediate and pressing Importance, unless suspended in their Operation till his Assent should be obtained; and when so suspended, he has utterly neglected to attend to them. HE has refused to pass other Laws for the Accommodation of large Districts of People, unless those People would relinquish the Right of Representation in the Legislature, a Right inestimable to them, and formidable to Tyrants only. HE has called together Legislative Bodies at Places unusual, uncomfortable, and distant from the Depository of their public Records, for the sole Purpose of fatiguing them into Compliance with his Measures. HE has dissolved Representative Houses repeatedly, for opposing with manly Firmness his Invasions on the Rights of the People. HE has refused for a long Time, after such Dissolutions, to cause others to be elected; whereby the Legislative Powers, incapable of the Annihilation, have returned to the People at large for their exercise; the State remaining in the mean time exposed to all the Dangers of Invasion from without, and the Convulsions within. HE has endeavoured to prevent the Population of these States; for that Purpose obstructing the Laws for Naturalization of Foreigners; refusing to pass others to encourage their Migrations hither, and raising the Conditions of new

Appropriations of Lands. HE has obstructed the Administration of Justice, by refusing his Assent to Laws for establishing Judiciary Powers. HE has made Judges dependent on his Will alone, for the Tenure of their Offices, and the Amount and Payment of their Salaries. HE has erected a Multitude of new Offices, and sent hither Swarms of Officers to harrass our People, and eat out their Substance. HE has kept among us, in Times of Peace, Standing Armies, without the consent of our Legislatures. HE has affected to render the Military independent of and superior to the Civil Power. HE has combined with others to subject us to a Jurisdiction foreign to our Constitution, and unacknowledged by our Laws; giving his Assent to their Acts of pretended Legislation: FOR quartering large Bodies of Armed Troops among us; FOR protecting them, by a mock Trial, from Punishment for any Murders which they should commit on the Inhabitants of these States: FOR cutting off our Trade with all Parts of the World: FOR imposing Taxes on us without our consent: FOR depriving us, in many Cases, of the Benefits of Trial by Jury: FOR transporting us beyond Seas to be tried for pretended Offences: FOR abolishing the free System of English Laws in a neighbouring Province, establishing therein an arbitrary Government, and enlarging its Boundaries, so as to render it at once an Example and fit Instrument for introducing the same absolute Rules into these Colonies: FOR taking away our Charters, abolishing our most valuable Laws, and altering fundamentally the Forms of our Governments: FOR suspending our own Legislatures, and declaring themselves invested with Power to legislate for us in all Cases whatsoever. HE has abdicated Government here, by declaring us out of his Protection and waging War against us. HE has plundered our Seas, ravaged our Coasts, burnt our Towns, and destroyed the Lives of our People. HE is, at this Time, transporting large Armies of foreign Mercenaries to compleat the Works of Death, Desolation, and Tyranny, already begun with circumstances of Cruelty and Perfidy, scarcely paralleled in the most barbarous

Ages, and totally unworthy the Head of a civilized Nation. HE has constrained our fellow Citizens taken Captive on the high Seas to bear Arms against their Country, to become the Executioners of their Friends and Brethren, or to fall themselves by their Hands. HE has excited domestic Insurrections amongst us, and has endeavoured to bring on the Inhabitants of our Frontiers, the merciless Indian Savages, whose known Rule of Warfare, is an undistinguished Destruction, of all Ages, Sexes and Conditions. IN every stage of these Oppressions we have Petitioned for Redress in the most humble Terms: Our repeated Petitions have been answered only by repeated Injury. A Prince, whose Character is thus marked by every act which may define a Tyrant, is unfit to be the Ruler of a free People. NOR have we been wanting in Attentions to our British Brethren. We have warned them from Time to Time of Attempts by their Legislature to extend an unwarrantable Jurisdiction over us. We have reminded them of the Circumstances of our Emigration and Settlement here. We have appealed to their native Justice and Magnanimity, and we have conjured them by the Ties of our common Kindred to disavow these Usurpations, which, would inevitably interrupt our Connections and Correspondence. They too have been deaf to the Voice of Justice and of Consanguinity. We must, therefore, acquiesce in the Necessity, which denounces our Separation, and hold them, as we hold the rest of Mankind, Enemies in War, in Peace, Friends. WE, therefore, the Representatives of the UNITED STATES OF AMERICA, in GENERAL CONGRESS, Assembled, appealing to the Supreme Judge of the World for the Rectitude of our Intentions, do, in the Name, and by Authority of the good People of these Colonies, solemnly Publish and Declare, That these United Colonies are, and of Right ought to be, FREE AND INDEPENDENT STATES; that they are absolved from all Allegiance to the British Crown, and that all political Connection between them and the State of Great-Britain, is and ought to be totally dissolved; and that as FREE AND INDEPENDENT STATES, they have full Power to levy War, conclude Peace, contract Alliances, establish Commerce, and to do all other Acts and Things which INDEPENDENT STATES may of right do. And for the support of this Declaration, with a firm Reliance on the Protection of divine Providence, we mutually pledge to each other our Lives, our Fortunes, and our sacred Honor.

John Hancock.

GEORGIA, Button Gwinnett, Lyman Hall, Geo. Walton.

NORTH-CAROLINA, Wm. Hooper, Joseph Hewes, John Penn.

SOUTH-CAROLINA, Edward Rutledge, Thos Heyward, junr., Thomas Lynch, junr., Arthur Middleton.

MARYLAND, Samuel Chase, Wm. Paca, Thos. Stone, Charles Carroll, of Carrollton.

VIRGINIA, George Wythe, Richard Henry Lee, Ths. Jefferson, Benja.Harrison, Thos. Nelson, jr., Francis Lightfoot Lee, Carter Braxton.

PENNSYLVANIA, Robt. Morris, Benjamin Rush, Benja. Franklin, John Morton, Geo. Clymer, Jas. Smith, Geo. Taylor, James Wilson, Geo. Ross.

DELAWARE, Caesar Rodney, Geo. Read.

NEW-YORK, Wm. Floyd, Phil. Livingston, Frank Lewis, Lewis Morris.

NEW-JERSEY, Richd. Stockton, Jno. Witherspoon, Fras. Hopkinson, John Hart, Abra. Clark.

NEW-HAMPSHIRE, Josiah Bartlett, Wm. Whipple, Matthew Thornton.

MASSACHUSETTS-BAY, Saml. Adams, John Adams, Robt. Treat Paine, Elbridge Gerry.

RHODE-ISLAND AND PROVIDENCE, C. Step. Hopkins, William

Ellery.

CONNECTICUT, Roger Sherman, Saml. Huntington, Wm. Williams, Oliver Wolcott.

IN CONGRESS, JANUARY 18, 1777.

Endorsements

Sid sits at the adult table with Will Rogers and Warren Buffet.

Jay Rosenberg,
Former Associate, Business Developer/Entrepreneur

A "must read" for anyone interested in the political scene. As usual, Sid Dinerstein calls them as he sees them and pulls no punches."

Tom Sliney,
former Chairman, Republican Party oPalm Beach County

Sid Dinerstein has always shown that a love of country stands above the love of a political party. This book shows all of how to hold both parties accountable to its citizens and how we can continue to have the best nation in the world. Read it and pass it on to a friend. Let's get our country back!

Harold P. Stern
County Commissioner

This is a" must read" for anyone that has common sense. His literary delivery is superb and unlike the norm his book delivers as promised: provocative, nonpartisan public policy. 'Adults Only' should be required reading for everyone, including at the high school level. If you LOVE this country... you'll LOVE this book!"

James A. Fantin
Mortgage Banker/President, Worth Mortgage Company

Sid's provocative wit and straight-talking style coupled with his seductive political knowledge and savvy make this book a "must read" for anyone who cares about their country and the issues we are facing. "Adults Only" is simply irresistible!

Lisa Marie Macci,

Esq., Syndicated Talk Radio Host, THE JUSTICE HOUR

Interesting reading for the political junkie and mandatory reading for people who think there are no solutions left for the problems we face."

Susan Whelchel

Deputy Mayor Boca Raton, Florida

Sid Dinerstein has an acute political mind. His ideas are right on the money. His book is a "must read."

John D. Herrick, Treasurer,

Palm Beach County Republican Party

The easy way out for Americans is to become "unthinkingly" partisan with one political party or stick their head in the ground like an ostrich and go on with their life oblivious to the World around them. Unfortunately, too many Americans are doing this very thing and Sid's book will point out why we should get seriously involved as "American's" to save America as we know it… or we will lose it.

Al Cohen,

Managing Partner of Real Estate Development Company

Dinerstein's charismatic attitude shines through in "Adults Only." He is not afraid to tell it like it is—what politics needs is to grow up and look at the bigger picture. What is REALLY better for America: partisanship or unity? It is about time someone took a stand and pointed out what's wrong in America.

Joanna Cunningham,

Committeewoman, Florida Legislative Committee on Intergovernmental Relations

We are witnessing an era of American politics whereby the Blue State versus Red State mentality is ever-increasing in a manner that is detrimental to our Nation's continued growth and prosperity. Sid Dinerstein has very correctly identified the need to place National priorities above political loyalties. "Adults Only" is an accurate and thoughtful approach to healing our Nation's political rifts.

Marion D. Thorpe, Jr., M.D., M.P.H.,
Florida Congressional Candidate

Sid Dinerstein's book "Adults Only" should be on your "must read" list if you are bothered by the ultra-partisanship in today's politics. Sid combines an appreciation of bedrock American values with a magnetic way with words that has charmed the local press over the years.

Jack Merkl,
previous Florida Congressional candidate

I encourage all who have a passion for our country to read this book. Sid Dinerstein offers a fresh perspective of the political land-scape in our world today. It will educate you as to why we must be more involved in choosing our leaders in local, state and federal government positions, regardless of party affiliation. Challenging us, as citizens, to discipline ourselves to think in terms of what is best for us in our neighborhoods, towns, region and nation, as opposed to following the agendas of political parties and their candidates. Sort of a turn back to the past and embrace what our founding fathers actually wanted for the future of our nation and its people.

Mark K. Trueblood,
Vice-Mayor, Town of Mangonia Park, FL

For anyone exhausted by the incessant bickering in politics and the endless campaign – this is your book.

Charlie Fetscher,
President, Palms West Republican Club

I have known Sid Dinerstein over fifty years. I highly endorse his book. He is stepping up and outside party lines to engage all "adults." He is bringing us ideas, asking us to think innovatively, asking us to act. He writes with the best interest of America.

Eleanor S. Katz, LCSW
(Licensed Clinical Social Worker, State of Hawaii)

Sid Dinerstein is a man of intellect and insight into the "nuts and bolts" of grassroots politics. After more than ten years of being closely involved with Sid in the political arena, I am convinced that our democracy would be much better served if politicians (of any party) would read this book and follow his wise counsel!

Fran Hancock,
Palm Beach County Committeewoman

Hopefully the title of the book will entice our young people to slip our of their bedrooms one night, tip toe down the stairs and take the book from their parents' book nook and run back to their room for real interesting reading.

Dr. Jerry Cammarata,
Former Commissioner New York City Department Of
Youth And Community Development

Sid Dinerstein's excellent book "Adults Only" points out how one major building block of our democracy has been eroding – the ability of Americans to come together as a people to solve the nation's problems. Bravo for having the courage to tell everyone that "democracy is not a spectator sport" and to offer solutions for a brighter future.

Maria Mamlouk,
Former State Department (USAID) Official

Sid starts with three issues where there is general agreement across party lines so most of his readers are on board for the harder choices necessary for serious adults to make if we are to have political comity in our country. Partisanship is running amuck — this book is an attempt to tame the animosity with a mature sense of responsibility. It promises to have the gratitude of posterity, for it is our children who pay the price for the profligate vote-buying today.

George Blumel,
Grandfather

Sid Dinerstein

About the Author

Sid Dinerstein is a businessman, civic leader, elected School Board official and major political party principal who knows America from the ground up.

Born and raised in Brooklyn, New York, Sid spent much of his adult life in Northern New Jersey. He has lived in South Florida for the past 17 years.

A graduate from Brooklyn College in 1966, Sid earned his BA in Economics before his 20th birthday, and was awarded his M.B.A. from City College of New York at the age of 21. After college he entered the business world and built JBS Associates, Inc., a financial service company, from a two-man operation in 1975 to a 600 employee private company by 1992. He was elected to two three-year terms on his local School Board in Ringwood, New Jersey and twice served as Board President. While in New Jersey, he coached softball, basketball and field hockey teams for young girls, and started his town's Recreation Girls' Basketball League.

Shortly after moving to South Florida, Sid became a fixture in Palm Beach County politics as chairman of the local Republican Party. He regularly weighs in on local and national policy issues through his extensive media relationships. Through his weekly radio talk show on WPBR, he focuses totally on the issue of Education and is the local informal Charter School Advocate. He currently chairs Palm Beach County's Palm Tran Advisory Board, a group that has increased the number of transit bus passengers more than 50 percent during his tenure without adding staff or buses.

Sid is the ultimate outsider in the current American political environment, solving real community problems without looking to Washington for help.

He has been married to the same woman for 40 years. He and Esther have two daughters and two granddaughters.

About this book, Dinerstein says, "It comes out of a fundamental truth that stares me in the face every day: Lord Acton was right when he said, 'Power corrupts. Absolute power corrupts absolutely.' Realizing that Lord Acton was right, across party lines, led to the writing of *Adults Only*... an effort to retrieve lost power on behalf of the citizenry."

Share *Adults Only* With Others

To order individual copies (less than 100) of the book:
Call 1-888-281-5170, M-F, 8-5 CST
Also available at:

Local bookstores
Amazon.com
www.siddinerstein.com

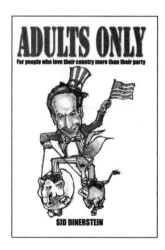

or contact:

QP Distribution
22167 C Street
Winfield, KS 67156
(888) 281-5170
Fax: (620) 229-8270

Adults Only, ISBN 978-1-884886-86-7
$15 ea + $6.75 shipping & handling (1-3 copies)

Customized books are available in bulk orders at special rates for sales promotions, premiums, fund-raising, or educational use.

Special editions can be created for specific needs. Contact StarGroup International for bulk quantities of 100 or more, as well as details on customized editions of 1,000 minimum.

StarGroup International
1194 Old Dixie Highway
Suite 201
West Palm Beach, FL 33403

(561) 547-0667
www.stargroupinternational.com